YOUR
SOCIAL STARTUP

A Step-By-Step Guide On How To Identify And
Start A Business You Love Within 30 Days And
Make The World A Better Place

Elena Lori

Dedicated to my parents.

The money raised from selling this book goes to financing social initiatives at BEL MONDO Ventures.

Minsk, 2016

PREFACE

This book is a tutorial designed for people who want to start their own mission-driven business, and for entrepreneurs who want to make their business more socially and environmentally conscious and more structured. In addition, this book will be useful for people who are looking for purpose in their life, who want to bring more meaning to their daily routine. The book begins by addressing the questions of purpose and motivation and then proceeds to the study of business creation tools. If you intend to become the independent creator of your bright and fulfilled life, this book is for you. Everything is broken down into 15 chapters, each chapter with its own task for you to complete. As you progress through the book, you will create your social start-up!

All the exercises in this book are developed and tested by the author.

Your Social Startup

Chapter 1
YOU

When you are happy, you are not questioning the purpose of life

Dear reader, I am very inspired to share the knowledge and skills on how to do things you love, help neighbours, and live a happy life. This is a book for good-makers - for people whose main desire is to help others and make the world a better place. If that includes you - congratulations! I admire people who want to help others. These are truly great people who have inner integrity, courage, generosity, and the drive of creators. My dream is this book will help you to learn to organize yourself in a way that you enjoy what you work on, prosper, and share this good energy with others! Doing business is difficult at times, it is a path with many challenges and hard tasks, but if you are doing things you love - then in critical situations you have the additional resources of energy, joy, strength, forgiveness, and what is more, you become steadfast in your inner confidence!

If someone who you love, or even someone unfamiliar are going through a hard time - how good it is to see them and wish them all the best, to tell them their presence and happiness are important to you, to help as much as you can. By doing this, we give more energy and joy to them, but also to ourselves. What if did this every day, constantly opening and increasing our potential and skills by helping others, making conscious actions of love in every moment?

Oh, how incredibly beautiful you will become in this quest for a happy, free, harmonious, and prosperous life for yourself and others!

After all, you are so special in your perfectionism and in your imperfections, in your sensitivity and stubbornness, in your openness and scepticism, in your uncertainty and belief, in your ease and playfulness, in your seriousness and boldness, in your modesty, in your progress and stability, in the work of your hands, in the stream of your

thoughts, in the pure intention of your soul, in your dreams, in your power, in your knowledge!

Realize that and enter the temple of your heart.

Show the world what you can be by simply rejoicing in your natural activities and pleasing the people who love you!

Other ways of life, where you are not you, are just not interesting. It is boring to spend precious days without moving, developing, or feeling the taste of life when you can do so much more. It is your life, but it will pass you by as you sit there waiting for the nice weather to come, or for some undefined miracle you can't logically predict...

Perhaps now you know how far you stand from the full realization of your potential, from a profound, happy, fulfilling life. In fact, this distance might suddenly make you become very sad. In this case, go down to the very depths of your despair, of your sufferings, pain, and powerlessness. Live it and feel it as much as possible. Experience the severity of your feelings and sadness as you see these conditions which chain you to the ground.

Now let go of this ballast. Set free all those who hurt you and forgive yourself for the adoption of this pain and for agreeing to preserve it in you. Burn yourself in the fire and free yourself from helplessness, fear, constraint, resentment, inferiority, insecurity, suffering, and frustration. Let the wind scatter the ashes...

It's time to for your soul to be reborn, to rise and shine!!! It's time to draw a new picture of you and your world on a blank sheet, a new image that you really like. Write which qualities and new feelings you want to develop in yourself. Do not constrain yourself – wish for the very best and most beautiful things which only you can imagine. For now, do not think how you can achieve this. It is important that you are on the right track!

Understand what just happened.

Only one moment separated you from a happy life, only one moment turned your attitude from a victim of life to a creator of life. A moment ago, you were sad and suffering, and now you rejoice. Now you are full of strength and energy! Perhaps it even feels silly that you were so tormented just a moment ago? Suffering is vanity, but we have chosen it in order to feel the fullness of life. This choice is always ours, the choice of the angle at which we perceive reality.

However, if we are to create a beautiful world, it is more practical to keep ourselves filled with energy. Energy is joy, love, intelligence, and beauty. This is the power to unite, to co-create something new and perfect, at first in the mind, and then on paper and in reality! Moreover, we intend to share this joy, health, beauty, and love with others, transforming it into perfect products and services. For that, we must try to create this usable energy in our thoughts, and fill ourselves with it through observing the beauty and logic of all that exists. And we should keep our soul clean of all unnecessary and heavy things.

If you did not experience any torment and anguish from the thought that life is passing by - congratulations! You are already on the right track! You only need to strengthen some components of your activity!

This book consists of 15 chapters. Each chapter contains a specific task to work through, aimed at the development of your business. The first chapters are devoted to understanding the fundamentals of your business and developing a strategy. Subsequent chapters are more hands-on and tell you what to do right now and how to do it. You will have to undertake a lot of work in order to shed light on all aspects of your future activities and work out new qualities in yourself. Be ready to have real start-up intensity! As stated before, each chapter has a task. After you complete it, put a tick in the box at the end of the chapter. Upon successful completion of all the tasks, you will create your favourite start-up which is useful to many!

The goal of this first chapter is to better understand yourself, your beauty, and your perfection, because only by grounding yourself on the beauty and strength inside, can you reveal or transcend it outside. Become yourself, synchronized with your true nature. Enjoy yourself and people around you will enjoy you, too. Stand in the position of the creator of your life, and you will not have contradictions or obstacles in the implementation of your plans. This chapter is the most important in the book, because it sets the framework, the very foundation on which to build your business, try to feel and understand it profoundly. It is all about your unconditional uniqueness, beauty, and potential.

☐ I intend to live a happy, harmonious, beautiful, healthy, prosperous life, bringing maximum benefit to myself and others.

Chapter 2
ON MISSION

Remain beautiful

Mission - it is something big and immense; it is the intention aimed at infinity. When choosing the work of your life, it would be good to define this foundation. Having a mission helps us in situations of uncertainty. Then we can consult with our mission to see if our actions are aligned with it and eliminate any fear, knowing we are on the best possible track that we consciously chose.

There are many techniques to determine your life purpose and the type of activity which is good for you. I propose my three-step method:

Step 1: Understand what you already have and what you consist of. In order to do so, you must split yourself into a number of qualities and states to determine which of them are your strongest and nicest – the ones you would willingly share with others. Remember, we are talking about spiritual qualities and qualities of character. The rule is the more of them you share, the more they grow. So, focus on what qualities you would like to grow and share. This will be also the main mechanism for our business. Here is my example:

My mission in life - to continuously build all this in myself and share it with others. Now you try. Fill in these circles with the qualities you are sure you possess, that delight you, that you would like to grow a little more, and share with others. You can draw even more circles! Believe me, nothing would make me happier.

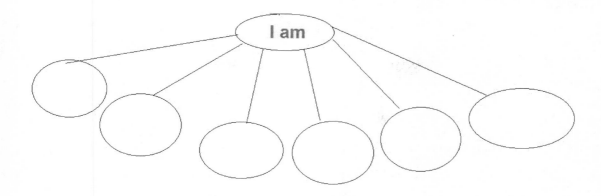

Finished? Excellent! Now, choose your most favourite one from these circles, the one that you want to share the most. Select the circle with which you are going to work, then think about and put your energy into it so that it grows with vigour and new knowledge. Once you've made your choice, continue to the next step.

Step 2: Now you must determine the direction of your influence. Who can benefit from what you have? Who would you like to do something good for the most? Select a number of very specific categories, from general to more narrow. Just think about who really needs this treasure the most. Who will feel good receiving it?

Here are some options for those you can share with. Select yours from the list or add your own: nature / people / companies / buildings / new-born babies / students / teenagers / lovers / families / orphans / seniors / students / entrepreneurs / unhealthy people / depressive people / searching people / doctors / teachers / people my from my neighbourhood / people of my city / pets / the disabled / other

_____

Step 3: Through which tools and instruments can you deliver what you have to those who need it? What are your abilities and skills? What have you learned? What is your education? What is your expertise? What can you be really great at after some practice? What would you really love to learn and excel doing in your life? Where did you work in the past and what knowledge and skills did you acquire?

Here are some options. Choose from the list or add your own. Just make sure you select your favourite activity: dancing / writing / public speaking / music / painting / work with hands / website development / website promotion / media / financial management / construction / training / consulting / project management / creation of a good team/ state service/ drawing up a marketing plan / growing plants / knowledge of chemistry / photography / programming / quality control / sports/ other

_____

After completing these three steps, we have a matrix from which we can combine the various options with ideas for your business. Complete this sentence: **I intend to share (Step 1) with (Step 2) by (Step 3)**. For example, "I intend to share love with entrepreneurs through teaching them" or "I intend to share health with the conscious people of my city by creating a team of like-minded farmers."

If the purpose of your business is to make the world better or to help people, it would be useful to look at the list of global humanitarian problems and at the relevant objectives identified by the UN Millennium Declaration to create a sustainable, harmonious world. I recommend acquainting yourself with a detailed description of each target at the UN website, which provides interesting facts and figures for each to explain why the objective is important. There are 17:

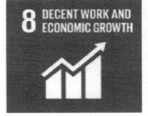

Write down what your options are, pick one, and we will continue polishing and refining it in the following chapters.

☐ I intend to share_____ with _____ _____ through_____.

My activity contributes to sustainable development by helping to achieve UN goal № __ "_____".

Chapter 3
ON STRATEGY AND TACTICS

To understand and embrace it - divide and conquer

Congratulations! We have created a generic vision of what we want to do and sketched out a rough idea. There may be many options, but let's choose one and pass it through the implementation. Throughout the following chapters we will explore and hone all the components that are necessary for a successful business.

Remember what we did to define our mission? We used the approach of isolating one quality from our holistic being that we are going to share with the world. After that we formed some general concept of our business. For example, I got something like, "**I intend to share love with entrepreneurs through teaching.**" Now, let's give a name to our future project. Choose a name which contains the essence of your business. I am going to use the name "BEL MONDO" for my company, which translates from Italian as "A Beautiful World."

Now, let's repeat the activity and divide our holistic business concept into a number of elements so we can analyse them separately. The elements of our business are as follows: Marketing, Product, Finance, Personnel, and Administration.

For your project, I recommend you create a folder on your computer or in Google Docs and name it as your project. Inside this folder, please create five sub-folders and name them: Marketing, Product, Finance, Personnel, and Administration. Now, for each of these five large fields we are going to create some larger strategic objective so that upon achieving these objectives, our project will be implemented. Having reached perfection in these five areas we will achieve excellence in our business. And by achieving excellence in our business, we are implementing the chosen mission of our life and realizing ourselves, because we are approaching our job as a harmonious continuation of Who I Am.

Here is an example of how to identify the intention for each of these five elements:

Mission	**BEL MONDO** *share love with entrepreneurs through education*				
	Product	**Marketing**	**Personnel**	**Finance**	**Administration**
Strategy	Create a digital platform where entrepreneurs can receive motivation, knowledge, tools and resources for developing their business.	Help 100.000 people in realizing their entrepreneurial initiatives.	Form the team of professional, loving, creative people	Achieve financial sustainability for the company and high salaries for people.	Create scalable, organized, transparent, inspirational system of company's management.
Tactics					

To fill in this table you will have to think really hard about HOW to solve the big challenge you set for each category.

A narrowly specialized intention specifically for the Product / Service, Marketing, Finance, Personnel, and Administration is our **strategy**. The sections of Product and Marketing are a showcase of our business, something that will be seen by our customers and partners. The sections Personnel, Finance, and Administration are our rear, and thanks to them, our business will be implemented.

After determining the strategic objectives for each area of our business, we continue our exercise of breaking down bigger components into smaller bricks, or things-to-do. These things-to-do will be our tactical steps.

To effectively develop an action plan, you need to gather the most comprehensive information on every aspect of your business. Google can help you explore the best practices of marketing, products, and so on in your specific industry!

For example, the tactical tasks would look something like this:

Product / Service: This is where you record everything that relates directly to the solutions of the problem you're going to offer your target audience. In this step, you need to have precisely defined and clearly visualized concept of what the product will be, what size, shape, colour, content, quantity, material, language, duration, etc.

At this stage, you should actively involve brainstorming techniques. Sketch all the possible options for solving the problem out on paper, analyse them all, drop some, and keep some for further polishing and research.

Here are examples of some of my tactical tasks on the Product:

- Decide on the main sections of a digital resource.
- Create functional and technical specification for the development of a resource.
- Decide on a colour palette for all the materials I will use in communications.
- Decide on the design of my web resource.
- Visualize server structure of the web application.

And so forth, the more detailed - the better! In the Product / Service section you should have at least 30 goals, elaborating on every function and its aspect.

Marketing: This relates to the outside world, namely, the target audience that you will engage as well as the analysis of competitive offerings. You must clearly understand who your client is, where he lives, what is going on in his life on daily basis, how it relates to various events, products, services that he checks, what he dreams about, how he handles this problem nowadays, and why he chooses particular companies and services. In marketing, you also need to decide on ways to come into contact with your client (be it a website, store, TV, trainings, videos, or other options).

Here are some examples of tactical objectives Marketing:

- Carry out a survey of people who dream about becoming entrepreneurs. Discover what information they lack, what problems they have, and whether they would be interested in my product. To do this, create a questionnaire.
- Create a database of institutions and resources that work with entrepreneurs and conduct marketing research with them based on my questionnaire.
- Develop a plan to promote information resources on the Internet (here comes a detailed description of all the options that you already know or that you researched as best practices for your niche: evaluate options of SEO promotion, a database of target contacts, accounts in social networks, blogs, radio, TV, club system, monthly subscription, etc.)

Of course, experienced entrepreneurs can quickly figure out which tools work and how to implement them, but if you are a beginner, your main assistant now is scrupulous research on Google, in books, and from the advice of highly specialized experts. Ask questions about how to implement the strategy you nailed for a particular activity. Set yourself the task of how you can interview your prospective clients about your solution.

Personnel: In this section, you must thoroughly think through all aspects of your work with the team. Who are they (employees, volunteers, freelancers), what is an example of their potential work schedule for the implementation, what tasks they will be responsible for, what results should they show, how will they learn, what character traits in them matter for you, and what experiences will it be important for them to have.

Here are examples of tasks:

- Create a description of the tasks you want to delegate.
- Create a list of requirements for each employee.
- Create a list of what you can offer in exchange for the work.
- Create performance benchmarks for each employee.
- Decide on what the staff needs in terms of equipment, methodologies, technology, guidelines, and special programs.

Finance: Here we describe all the challenges associated with numbers, such as the cost of services, the assets available, one-time and permanent costs, break-even point analysis, and correspondent financial goals.

Examples of tasks:

- Create a plan of expenses for production and sales of the product.
- Plan the necessary volume of the product to reach financial sustainability/break-even.
- Create a portrait of an ideal investor.
- Create a list of potential investors.

Administration: This section will be dedicated to everything that creates the management structure and framework of your business. It includes all legal issues (all kinds of necessary legal documents), rent matters, all the rules and regulations of doing business, organizational structure, strategy and tactics, automation tools, and methodologies.

Examples of tasks:

- Select a web-based task management system,
- Formulate and ensure a quality control process,

- Provide a convenient document storage system,
- Organize accounting books,
- Introduce the practices of a healthy lifestyle,
- Find a mentor.

Your assignment for this chapter is to find a big piece of drawing paper, markers, pens, and paper stickers of different colours, then write the mission of your business strategy and place the stickers for tactical tasks in the correct place. Please note that tactical tasks should have no less than 100 things-to-do! Also, at this stage it is very useful to receive advice from successful entrepreneurs, business coaches, mentors, and experts in your business in order to properly approach strategic and tactical objectives. Assigning the tasks correctly is a half job done for creating your business.

Here is a sample template for your planning:

Mission					
	Product	**Marketing**	**Personnel**	**Finance**	**Administration**
Strategy					
Tactics					

In the course of your activities, your mission should remain unshakable and will be the basis of everything. Your strategy will vary a little and be expanded based on your new understanding.

Tactics - this is a constantly changing field, with supplementing and successfully implemented elements. The strategy and tactics should be regularly reviewed, especially in the early phase of the project, when you experiment and test different niches, tools, and approaches and this should go on until the phase when you have developed a stable, operating business.

☐ I am clearly aware of the mission of my project. I developed the strategy and tactics of its implementation.

Chapter 4
ON GOALS AND IMPACT

You are the creator, so what will you build, really?

The concept of doing business that I suggest is called the "triple bottom line". It is a hybrid between business and charity. The task of any classic business is profit maximization, and the task of any classic charity is to maximize positive social and environmental effects. So, in our model, we practice a mixed approach. This means we seek to maximize the number of paid contracts with customers and then use the received dividends to maximize charitable effects. The base for our model is our desire for a better world, and our desire to deliver the solution for social and environmental challenges.

Why it is not enough just to do business, creating positive products and services and selling them to anyone who can afford them? In the classic business, owners and investors think only about how to sell more and how to meet the interests of people and companies who have finance. This creates a vicious circle - the rich get richer and the poor get poorer. This happens because our modern financial system is built on the principle of a pyramid, or a control centre, where 99% of the financial resources are entrusted to 1% of people, or organizations run by these people. Hacking this system and climbing to the top of the pyramid is a difficult task and often of Sisyphean work and great compromise. And even if you do achieve it, you will be in the 1% of these people, while your friends, those closest to you, and strangers will not cope and win in this race of ants, bears, and jaguars for the title of the world champion in running.

The definition of success and wealth is actively proposed to us in the media; however, who said that it is suitable to everyone? Do you want to burn so much energy and time if, as an alternative, you could just create and gradually expand your little paradise, filling it with the joy of creativity, appreciation, love, sincere gratitude, and loyal friends? After all, you can take what you already have right now on the spot and fill every moment and every centimetre of space with your conscious attention, beauty, and love instead of ignoring, or, in the worst case, sacrificing it for the sake of the big and unknown. With such a foundation, won't you be able to realize the image of the life of your dreams and become a truly happy and prosperous person? You, as a creator, entrepreneur, and rule setter, can get out of a system that is not quite right for you, and create an alternative one, based on your deepest values and needs and compliant with your environment.

Now consider the second option. Why not engage in pure charity, to create a classic non-profit company (NGO), not to sell any services, and leave your funding at the mercy of your sponsors? Then you would have a lot of free time to focus on helping those in need. Many people who wish to engage in socially useful projects have this thought in their brain that earning money is something low; however, they accept donations and sponsorship. But if you think about this sponsorship and where it comes from, you quickly realize many of the wealthiest sponsors who finance you create their capital out of the existing system we live in, which has a lot of environmental, social, and financial gaps. For this company to continuously support you, it will have to keep up the pace of business and continue to destroy the surface of the earth or, overall, any old-fashioned, unsustainable, but profitable activities. In this case, you are indirectly supporting the system. Isn't it just easier to provide your own personally developed services to those who need them and who have at least some money to pay for them, rather than deciding to hang on sponsors?

Thus, in my opinion, the best way of doing things is to have a company that sells **useful** products or services, and then, at the expense of its own profits finances its own charitable action. Although, of course, the choice is yours. I suggest you don't categorize decisions, though, because there are many fine examples of classic businesses and classical NGOs, which do a lot of good for themselves and for the people around them. Moreover, if you already have a base, for example, your own business or an NGO, it is much more constructive to develop and modify it, starting from what is already there. That being said, it is useful to keep in mind your intention for continuous harmonization of the business and try different options to expand its positive impact, while reducing dependencies.

Sometimes it happens that a company is barely making ends meet or making any profit. In this case, to create social and environmental impact, think about what you can do or share with little or no money. This may, for example, be:

- Providing some useful information, tools, or research in an open free access;
- Introducing healthy lifestyle practices, consumption of quality water, or a break for physical activity in your company;
- Mechanisms to encourage the team to carry out charitable visits, work, or fundraising;
- Eco-friendly practices in the handling of materials: reuse, reduce consumption, recycle;
- Paperless office and document management;
- Reducing electricity consumption through the use of energy efficient equipment: energy-saving light bulbs, computers, servers that run on solar and wind energy;
- Reducing gasoline consumption in the company, giving preference to walks, biking, or car sharing practices;
- Encouraging practices of video conferencing, online training, working from home as a more effective means of organizing business, saving time, and saving resources to commute, and getting better service;
- Providing freedom and opportunities for employees to implement their own initiatives, the promotion of creativity, and follow-up on implementation;
- Giving preference to banks that support social initiatives;
- Employing people with disabilities;
- Developing and adhering to the ethical code of conduct for employees and owners of the company; making important decisions based on the universal values of health, happiness, prosperity, and freedom.

If you liked any of these initiatives, add them to the strategy and tactics you developed in the last chapter.

So, to start your business, you need to set goals to achieve and create an action plan. In the triple-bottom-line concept, we set targets in three areas:

- social effect,
- profitability,
- environmental effect.

Social and environmental effects should be expressed in specific numbers (metrics), or describe a qualitative change/transition.

Here are the examples of the most common metrics:

- The number of people on a monthly basis (or lump sum) receiving charitable help from your case;
- The number of products you transferred to charitable causes;
- The number of people informed about the social problems you decide - the media coverage;
- A qualitative change in the composition of the materials used, and how it affects the health and well-being of people.
- A qualitative change in people's access to information, which helps to improve their health and well-being.

There is a special organization called the IRIS which develops metrics. Setting your target metrics allows you to see which direction you need to grow. Also, with these numbers you can better present your company and the impact of its activities to clients, sponsors, investors, partners, and the general audience.

Now, create a document called "Business Objectives" in the "Administration" folder and complete it based on Examples 1 and 2. All the figures in the examples are random.

Part 1: Metrics of Social and Environmental Impact

Example 1: Directions to maximize the positive impact of the project "producing hospital covers for premature babies":

№	Metric	Goal (period 1 Jun 2016- 1 Jan 2017)	Result
1	Number of covers produced	60	
2	Number of engaged hospitals which received aid	10	
3	Number of children/recipients of the aid	From 40 to 120 children per month	
4	Percentage of the need of these covers addressed in Belarus (on country level)	50%	
5	Media outreach (audience)	100.000 persons	
6	Used material	100% ecological	

7	Number of disabled people who received a job thanks to this project	2 persons	
8	Number of volunteers engaged		
9	Something else which is good and can be presented in numbers		

Your job as a social entrepreneur will be to figure out how to grow these metrics. You should plan these concrete numbers based on the resources you have at your disposal now.

Part 2: Financial Sustainability.

You need to calculate what costs you have (including your own salary) in order to deliver your impact. Based on that, you should design a list of services which would allow you to finance your impact and calculate the necessary amount of their realization. With that approach, your business will ensure compliance with social and environmental metrics and at the same time will become self-financed without having to depend on sponsors.

Example 2: Brainstorming the areas of maximizing the financial viability of the project "Tailoring the covers for premature babies."

Costs - Purchase of material, wages, rent, depreciation of equipment, travel expenses, advertising. The necessary budget to implement social effect - 5000 USD with the duration of 3 months.

№	Idea	How realistic it is, nuances, plusses, and minuses	Planned revenue, USD	Planned profit, USD
1	Sell own products of similar type through social networks, mentioning that 10% goes to charitable purpose.	Already works. Next steps: advertising in social networks, work with journalists.	3000	300
2	Allow the hospitals to finance the covers themselves.	Create a database of hospitals and ask them if they are ready to buy goods now or in future, who is responsible.	0-1000	0-1000
3	Sell own products through fundraising platforms similar to Kickstarter	Create and publish a project, promote it	3000	1500

4	Sign contracts for goods distribution in popular supermarket chains	Not realistic within next 3 months with the current production volume. Make a special certification, make a database of the chains, hold negotiations. Allocate a separate budget for certification	20000	5000
5	Attract a corporate sponsor	Create a database of companies, create a project pitch	2000	2000
6	Sell advertisement on your product	Create a database of companies which might be interested in this advertising, negotiate	3000	2000
7	Develop mini-souvenirs and sell them in local cafes.	Negotiate with cafes, develop a product, set up the price and the procedure of cash out.	3000	1500
8	Add a "donate" button on the website	Consult with a developer, lawyer, and the bank	0-1000	0-1000
9	Other initiatives for financing this venture			

	(contests, partnerships, etc.)			

Continue making this list until you ensure you will have enough revenue and profit to fulfil your goal even with the most pessimistic forecast.

Done? Perfect! If you have questions - write us.

Let's move on. Now is the time to put together all our intentions and make a plan, including when and how exactly we will accomplish it. Create a document titled "**Project Plan**" in the Administration folder and fill it in following the structure below.

Form 1: "Plan for Project ABC"

Description of task	Duration	Deadline	Resources (people, finance, etc.)	Comments
Fill in the document "Metrics of the business and financial sustainability"	1 day	1.11.2016	-	

Create a "Project Plan"	1 day	2.11.2016		
.....				

In order to fully complete this document, you should use all your tactical to-do things from the previous chapter and insert them in this plan. Move your sticky notes in this project plan. I recommend you have this plan in two forms: as a board with stickers and an electronic version. The board with stickers is very helpful for overviewing what goes well and what comes with obstacles. This way, you can quickly adjust your project plan or change their consequences. It is convenient to mark tasks which belong to particular categories Marketing, Product, etc. with separate colours.

The project plan should include a detailed description of the tactical goals. Moving further, you should be able to introduce this plan to your personnel and share the tasks between them.

In addition, there are different advanced tools for project planning and special software (for example, Microsoft Project, OpenProj, GanttProject, ProjectLibre). You can study them by yourself.

☐ I created the document "Metrics of business and financial sustainability" where I set my goals and elaborated on different channels for making money.

☐ I created the document "Project Plan" where I entered all the tasks for my business.

Chapter 5
ON ECOSYSTEM

Realize you are in a matrix, step out, and build your own

Now that you have quite a well thought out vision of you and your business, you should look at the ecosystem you are in. You should understand the basic rules of business for the participants and the niches where you want to go. Also, it is important to determine the direction in which the system is moving and developing. Like a new-born enters into society and develops in himself a number of traits and finds his best occupation, you should likewise tailor the role and place of your newly created business.

We all live in many systems at the same time. This is our culture, our climate system, a geographic system, economic system, and social system, as well as our views system - our perception of the world and self-awareness.

This chapter is devoted primarily to the study of socio-economic chains; however, I recommend you also do your own research on how other systems affect your business. Our goals for this research include:

- Understanding which companies and organizations are closest to our business and analyse the possibility of a partnership with them;
- Expand our understanding of how the problem was solved in the past (maybe even centuries ago), and what trends exist to address it in the future.

Let us study an example of the project "*Collection of expired drugs from citizens, and their safe disposal.*"

Let us map a few chains that exist now.

Chain 1: "The movement of a drug from its birth to death"

Option 1:

(1) The drug is created in the laboratory, tested, and approved -> (2) the drug is produced at a factory in our country or imported from abroad -> (3) the drug enters pharmacies -> (4) the drug is sold to patients -> (5) unused medicine goes to the dump along with other waste and then pollutes the soil and water, which causes poisoning and antibiotic resistance.

Main players: (1) Laboratory and state -> (2) plant -> (3) pharmacy-> (4) a citizen -> (5) landfill.

Option 2:

(1) The drug is created in the laboratory, tested, and approved -> (2) the drug is produced at a factory in our country or imported from abroad -> (3) the drug enters hospitals-> (4) The drug is given to patients by doctors under medical supervision -> (5) expired drugs are transferred for processing in a specially certified company, where they are burned in special circumstances so they are not harmful to the environment.

Main players: (1) Laboratory and state -> (2) plant -> (3) hospital-> (4) a doctor and a citizen -> (5) a specialized company for recycling.

The analysis suggests the following conclusions:

1. To date, the process by which people buy a drug in a pharmacy is quite harmful because people do not have the opportunity to dispose of the medicine properly, which creates an environmental problem.
2. However, the drug is also utilized in hospitals and processed by specialized recycling companies.
3. Therefore, it is worth considering the possibility of partnerships (!) with these members of the chain with an already existing infrastructure for the collection and disposal of medicines.
4. It is always cost effective and faster to create a partnership than to set up your own infrastructure from scratch. The task of a talented businessman is to bring all the partners together like a Lego constructor, and to stand in the middle of the process to include all the partners in the chain of movement of goods and finances.
5. If it turned out that there is no precedent for drugs being recycled, it would be necessary to go beyond our region. Thus, we would consider our process in the context of a broader geographic system. That is, if some problem cannot be solved in our village, perhaps

there is a way to solve it in the nearest town, or at the national, regional, and international levels. An alternative would be to evaluate the costs of setting up the entire infrastructure from scratch.

6. In this case, **our service** is somewhere on the level of the fourth element in our chain, the moment, after a person has acquired a drug in a pharmacy, but before he has disposed it. In order to solve the problem at this level, it is necessary to involve the nearby elements (3) and (5) in creating the solution. For example, we could talk to a pharmacy and suggest they organize a drug collection, or talk to trash collectors, suggesting they sort this type of waste. However, an in-depth look at the full (!) chain of a drug's life cycle suggests that the root of the problem actually lies deep in the foundation, i.e. directly at the element (1) when the chemical synthesis of a drug takes place and cannot be decomposed by a biological method. So, to resolve this problem at the root, we should work with further standing elements of the chain - with the laboratories by either inviting them to create a chemical process of de-synthesis and utilization of their medication, or in general, use only natural ingredients in production, which is a more harmonious way of interacting with the environment.

The methods of working with chains to solve problems are:

Transfer

With this approach, we need to find two different chains of the product life cycle. The first chain, in our case, is an ineffective one. But the second chain offers a solution. Therefore, we need to move the solution from the first to the second string. To do this, you need to bring in the players (3) and (5) of the second circuit. For the effective transfer, you need to come up with a different circuit from different industries, but which have similarities with your processes.

Deepening

Deepening is used when the surrounding components of the chain (in our case, 3 and 5, a pharmacy and a dump) refuse to accept the changes. In this case, we need to move deeper into the chain in all directions, talking about the problem with the importer and manufacturer of drugs as well as with the relevant regulators - state bodies or their assistants - lobbyists, and environmental organizations.

Reducing

The method of cutting the chain should be used where the chain is too long and is not optimal. In this case, your offer will be in how the participants of your chain can save time or money.

Expansion

Expansion of the chain means bringing in a new system of coordinates:

a) Geographical: in our example, we have considered the issue at the local level, it is necessary to examine the solutions at the national or global level.

b) Historical: consider how this issue has evolved in history. For example, if we examine the subject of bio products, we can see that 500 years ago, this problem did not exist, therefore the system can bring some mechanisms of the past into the chain.

c) Ideological: according to the Maslow pyramid, human needs vary from a material level to a more abstract and missionary level. Therefore, to solve the problem, we can use the arguments of either more down-to-earth or more idealistic and spiritual orders.

You can analyse and come up with other examples of chains that make a difference in the behaviour around the problem you are solving.

In this example project "Collection of expired drugs from citizens, and their safe disposal", we looked at only one chain, the movement of a drug from its birth to death.

For this project, one should also consider other chains, such as:

- Collection and disposal of waste (of all types);
- Collection of something from citizens (see existing chains which are collecting old clothes, gathering opinions, collecting financial donations, etc.);
- Public participation in other social and environmental initiatives.

As a result of our analysis, we find a lot of actors / organizations with whom we can build partnerships. In our case, this is a list of pharmacies, hospitals, and processing plants. In addition, we can cooperate with the administration of local communities, media, and environmental organizations.

Your task for this chapter will be to draw the chains in which your product or services participates. So you will find out who can be your closest partner, how the problem is already being solved, and what the root of the problem you solve is. Again, I recommend you use sticky notes for mapping the elements of your chains, because in this way you will be able to move these elements while developing your own vision of the problem and the chain you want to create.

Once you can handle your chains, you will be able to answer the question:

What exactly will YOUR service or products be?

You will also get responses to the following:

- Where can you find the material and resources for your product and services (where they are present in the chain)?
- Who will be able to pay for your product?
- Who can teach you the nuances of your industry?
- What is the market need for your services or products?
- What is a precise, narrow, clear cut offering you should start with in your business, and what do you need to strive for long term?

Most important, think which companies/members of the chain could be ready to enter long term agreements with you.

We live in times of rapid transformation of social, economic, and industrial systems. Many industries disappear or are transformed 360 degrees thanks to the processes of virtualization, remote business management, online training, automation, robotics, and other globalization trends. Many people do not keep up with these changes, lose their jobs, and need retraining. We should have a good understanding of these trends so we can base our business on the growing trends.

Here are some of the most interesting rising trends you can use in your business:

1. Circular economy - active use of the principles, where goods and services move in a circle a maximum number of times, and then get disposed in the most efficient and environmentally friendly way.
2. Sustainable development - the principles of equal attention to aspects such as social, environmental friendliness, and profitability as a base for harmonious development.
3. The principle of integrity, holistic development, and holistic approach - it implies that an individual or a company who understands the root of the problem can solve all the consequences, while specialization does not solve the problem at a fundamental level.
4. Crowdfunding - an approach to project financing, when the project prefers to have 100 sponsors of 10 dollars than one sponsor for 1000 dollars. Using crowdfunding is particularly useful for projects that produce the product in the B2C segment, available for pre-order.
5. Crowdsourcing - like crowdfunding, it involves only the collection and sourcing of any value from the crowd, for example, the collection of knowledge, opinions, labour, and other things.
6. Crowdsharing - when many people use one product or service collectively, for example, such as a car or a guided city tour.
7. Customization - the desire to have a unique product or service. This phenomenon is also called "the phenomenon of a long tail". It exists, for example, in music stores, where most of the sales occur for the album of one group, but behind this group there is a long tail which offers hundreds of bands, which are also sold and have their audience. This phenomenon also contributes to the growing

popularity of numerous clothing designers, furniture, and various customizable items, types of fabrics and other attributes that are actively used by major manufacturers to make each product a little different.

8. Natural, eco, bio - a growing desire of consumers to buy organic, natural foods. A special area in this niche - a superfood – is a type of product with the highest mineral and nutritional value, i.e., all sorts of bars made of natural nuts, seeds, herbal supplements. The global market of superfoods has exceeded $1 billion.

9. Ecological footprint (carbon footprint) - this is the principle that environmental impact is taken in mind by the enterprise, i.e., how much emissions are directly or indirectly produced by this company and what to do to reduce them. There are many small enterprises and alternative, clean energy providers in this domain, as well as companies that promote a more efficient use of transport.

10. Ethical business - a set of initiatives aimed at encouraging businesses to do good. This includes having a green policy and the Code of Ethics and all kinds of environmental certifications. You can also include the principle of fair trade, and the support of marginal groups and countries.

11. Corporate social responsibility - these are internal programs run by corporations to create social, environmental, and charity effects. However, during the implementation of these programs, a negative phenomenon called "green washing" (greenwashing) occurs. This is a situation in which the company tries to whiten their image to create public relations through the implementation of social initiatives, but avoids investing in harm reduction. For example, an oil company, damaging the environment and not investing in the elimination of oil spills, but leading in the ranking of the best job providers and best social packages.

12. Decentralization (horizontal economy) - a set of mechanisms, suggesting that any person or organization may receive early access to all resources, and they are not controlled by only a small group of people. Thus, the principle of a horizontal economy is supposed to give people all the necessary resources for their freedom, health, and well-being and abolish control mechanisms. Examples of such projects include small capacity power stations, when every home and the state as a whole becomes energy independent; a blockchain - decentralized financial system, not using the SWIFT central channel for money transfer; access to the best training materials online from anywhere in the world, etc.

Now that you have an idea about the system in which you work, it's time to go from conceptualization to implementation. Make a list of counterparties (potential customers, different types of partners) with whom you can interact. Now create a file titled "Potential Partners" and research on Google for at least ten companies in each category. Save the file in the "Marketing" folder.

Example 1:

Categories of partners for collaboration:

a) pharmacies

b) hospitals

c) waste processing enterprises

d) waste collecting enterprises

e) others..

№	Category	Name	Address	Contacts	Comments

In the next chapter we are going to learn how to establish contact with a potential partner with maximum efficiency.

☐ I created the file "Potential Partners" where I entered 100+ potential partners for my business from different categories.

☐ I found answers to the questions:

- Where can I find the material and resources for my product and services (where they are present in the chain)?
- Who will be able to pay for my product?
- Who can teach me the nuances of my industry?
- What is the market need for my services or products?
- What is a precise, narrow, clear cut offering I should start with in my business, and what do I need to strive for long term?

Chapter 6
ON A PITCH

Talk to people, unite with them, love them

In this chapter, we will finally communicate! It is time to pick up your phone and maybe even go to your first business meeting. The purpose of this chapter is to communicate with potential clients and partners, get their feedback on your project, gain knowledge about their practical experience in your field and, of course, collect the first agreements and pre-orders for future cooperation.

Step 1: Take the list of categories from the previous chapter and see which categories could be your potential customers, and which categories could provide you with resources for your products and services. For each category, you should have a substantial number of contacts (20-100) to process. To expand the list of potential customers, consider buying a database of companies with contacts in your target categories. For each category, create a one sentence proposal and a list of benefits that your service and product can provide specifically to them.

Example 1: "Production of ecological linen bags made by people with disabilities"

Category 1: Celebrities and sport stars

We would like to offer you the possibility to purchase ecological Belarusian souvenirs labelled with your own design, made with love by people with disabilities.

Advantage 1: Procure your own ecological souvenir product with a special design.

Advantage 2: Support the employment of people with disabilities.

Advantage 3: Help the disabled in their PR (public relations) campaign to promote their product.

Category 2: Supermarkets / Retailers of food

We would like to invite you to participate in the implementation of our eco-friendly reusable bags, made by people with disabilities, and to conduct a PR campaign.

Advantage 1: Implement a CSR program (Corporate Social Responsibility).

Advantage 2: Sell reusable bags for groceries.

Advantage 3: Conduct a contest of selfies with bags with a special hashtag for social networks as your supermarket advertising.

Advantage 4: Expand the range of products of local producers in your shop.

Advantage 5: Mark our reusable bags with your own logo

Advantage 6: Extend the coverage of your business in the media with the help of our social project.

Category 3: Gift Shops

Category 4: Online Gift Stores

...

Step 2: Start calling the contacts from the first category with the purpose of carrying out a marketing survey.

Here is an example of the speech for the call:

Greeting: "Good afternoon! "

Presentation of yourself and the project: "My name is Elena, I would like to present our project of reusable linen bags made by people with disabilities."

Question: "Can I talk to the Director / Chief Engineer / Head of Marketing (whoever suits you the most for your intended collaboration, or depending on the size of the company)? I would like to ask a few questions for our marketing research. It will take two minutes."

(After you have connected to the right person - repeat the past points again)

Pitch and the validation of the benefits (Here you need to make sure you have understood correctly the expectations of your target audience):

"I am conducting a market research. We would like to offer you the possibility to purchase ecological Belarusian souvenirs marked with your own design and made with love by people with disabilities."

- I wonder whether you liked the opportunity to buy your own ecological souvenir product with a special design? **Yes/ No. If no, ask why (this is very important!)**
- I wonder whether you are interested in supporting the employment of people with disabilities? **Yes/No**
- I wonder whether you would like to help people with disabilities in their PR campaign to promote their product? **Yes/ No**

Closing note: Thank you for your answers and your time. They will help us a lot. Can I connect with you on this project once again when we are ready to go ahead with it?

Step 3: In the last chapter you created a database of contacts for outgoing calls. Now, add to that table the following columns to the right: Feedback and Summary.

Mark the cells red in the column "Feedback" if the person/company is not interested in your offer, mark them green if interested, mark them orange if the answer is maybe, 50/50, or not so clear, and leave the cell white if you were unable to reach out to a decision maker to get your answers.

In the column "Summary" write down the points your contact made during the call - this is something you need to pay attention to in the preparation of your offer.

Keep making telephone calls to other categories. In the course of calling, be flexible about adjusting your pitch and adding new benefits you can offer to your contacts.

After receiving a negative answer, don't worry, just cross out a cell in the table below. A real passionate entrepreneur has a strong spirit and is able to withstand 100 "Nos". After all, you're doing this venture for yourself, you are on the very important quest of setting up the business of your love. However, be reasonable and prudent, if you see that the answer "no" is coming one after another, it may be necessary to step back, see where you made mistakes or didn't complete not enough work in the previous chapters. You might also want to reconsider your pitch, target categories, and the list of benefits. You might even need to go back to the beginning and try again. Perhaps the solution you are suggesting is not optimal for this problem, this time, or this audience. However, do hurry to such a pessimistic conclusion before you cross at least 100 Nos!

Your task during your calls to potential customers is to make sure that "no" is heard less and less. This means you have nailed the problem and the expected solution.

No	No	No	No	No	No	No	No	No	No
No	No	No	No	No	No	No	No	No	No
No	No	No	No	No	No	No	No	No	No
No	No	No	No	No	No	No	No	No	No
No	No	No	No	No	No	No	No	No	No
No	No	No	No	No	No	No	No	No	No
No	No	No	No	No	No	No	No	No	No
No	No	No	No	No	No	No	No	No	No
No	No	No	No	No	No	No	No	No	No
No	No	No	No	No	No	No	No	No	No

So, by the time all categories have been telephoned and studied properly, you will have a good idea of who needs your service needs and who will be the easiest bet to get you started. Now we can prepare an offer.

An offer is the essence of your business, a commercial offer is like the "business card" of your company. The offer addresses all the main questions: what you sell, who needs it, why, how it will work, how much it costs, and how it is delivered. The offer is the window case of your business.

The offer should be:

a) Fair;

b) Short;

c) Concrete.

Position your service or product in a way that you can do business on a permanent basis. For example, create a monthly service, subscription, monthly updates, regular orders, or new coming programs. If you can do this, it will significantly simplify the work because you won't need to look hard for new clients anymore. If you managed to do this and concluded a long-term contract, you do not have to worry about selling again and looking for new customers. You only need to focus on adding value and satisfaction to your current customers.

For example, you sell training services. Instead of trying to close a single deal, tell them that you have a themed 1-day educational course for each month of the year. So, if they like your work, they will remain with you to keep up-to-date on the courses.

So, in order to create a quality and good looking professional offer, you need to find a nice template and customize it with your data. To do this, I recommend using the following software:

Google Docs - they have a templates gallery for different purposes. Choose what pleases you and remake it for yourself. The gallery with documents' templates looks like this:

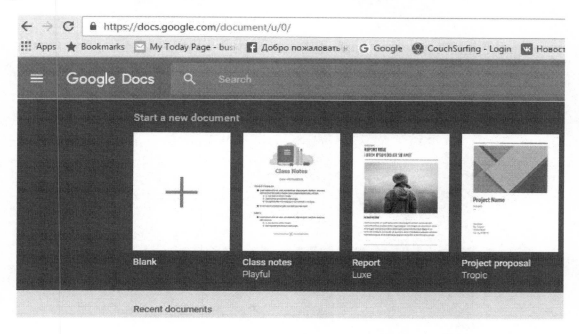

I usually choose the templates "Report" or "Project Proposal". Put a nice illustrative image at the beginning of the document and then add a paragraph on each of the sections: "About", "How it works", "Price and terms", "Benefits", "About us", and "Contact us."

Also, you can create an one-page fancy offer which looks like a infographic and points out all the important information. For that you can use, for example, Canva.com templates:

I completed a mini market research, and called over 100 potential customers from different categories. Based on the responses received, I modified the vision of my business. As a result, less people tell me "no". I collected 100 "no's" and thus became a real connoisseur of my business. I built a clear understanding of who is interested in my products and services and in what form.

> ☐   I developed a professional offer. Now I know for sure that people need my product or service!

Chapter 7
ON BRANDING

Again, it is about beauty

For professional work with partners and customers, you need to create your brand.

These are the aspects of branding we will address in this chapter:

- Company name;
- Tagline;

- Logo;
- The name of the web site (domain);
- Creating a website;
- Colour palette;
- Business card.

All these challenges should be resolved in two days with little or no investment.

The first question is whether you're going to create your own brand, or use someone else's brand name for your work?

There are many reason why it might be easier to take advantage of a partner's brand:

1. **Your business is a franchise of an existing project.** There are plenty of ready-made social and environmental projects that can be implemented in your city/country. I created a catalogue of such social franchises on my website: http://belmondoventures.com/start-your-impact-venture/

2. **It will be easier for you to implement your business with a partner who has a known brand and significant accumulated audience.** For example, if you want to offer the services of custom software development for social and charitable projects, you may find it easier to find a partner who is already engaged in custom software development and use his brand name for the implementation and promotion of your niche initiatives. In addition, such an experience would help you to understand all the nuances of a new business without any risk.

If these options are not relevant for you, then let's get started with developing your brand from the ground up!

1. Company name

As the ship moves the way it is called, so try to name your business in a beautiful way. The name should express your mission and, preferably, should be easy to remember. And another small detail, if the name starts with the first letter of the alphabet, then your company will always be at the top of all lists, rankings, lists of conference participants, and accordingly, will receive greater visibility. But it's not critical.

Write down a column with 10 name options and choose the one!

2. Tagline

The tagline should be the soul of your venture and should consist of 3-4 words that might convey the basic idea of your business. Go back to the second chapter, remember what quality of your soul you chose to implement in your business and make it into a slogan.

3. Logo

The logo should express the intent of your business in the form of a character, an alphabetic code, or a graphic element.

If you no skills whatsoever with design - no problem! With the help of Canva.com you can create a great logo in five minutes for free. Go to the web site, open a blank form, and move the necessary elements to it, or make an inscription with the help of the beautiful fonts and headers available. At Canva.com there is a huge database of all sorts of icons and elements, but even if something is missing, you can download an icon or image from your computer and use it as a design element. Save and download the completed image - the logo is ready! Time spent - 10 minutes, budget - $0.

4. The name of the web site - domain.

There are many sites for a domain search, one of the most popular is godaddy.com. Go there and enter the name of the site you want and see which domains are available. Domains in the .com zone are becoming scarce and more expensive, so consider domains with interesting extensions, for example, .people, .club, .charity, and others. They are much cheaper, and there is no reason to ignore them. The site will work fine on any domain, a domain name is only a matter of euphony.

Try to avoid the names of sites with hyphens, underscores, and periods because it will be difficult for you to pronounce your website when you talk with people. This might bring problems when you dictate the name of your site on the phone, because people often make mistakes in remembering sites with compound names. The cost of a domain is usually around $10 per year. If you want to save that $10, then look for options of free domains. Keep in mind, however they will have long, awkward names.

5. Create a web site

To quickly create a website, I recommend using such platforms as wordpress.com or wix.com. You do not need to be a programmer for this. There is a free website constructor at these platforms. If the software is not the foundation of your business, then the most important thing in your case is simplicity. Choose the easiest pattern to logically arrange all the important info in neat sections.

Also, your site will take up some space on the server machines, where it will be stored. This service is called hosting. Website hosting costs are around $50-$100 per year. Look for contacts of hosting providers located in your town. Hosting can also be purchased directly at wordpress.com and wix.com if you decide to use them. You can also take advantage of free hosting, although this option contains limitations. If you are a geek, you can make a server out of your own computer and host a website there.

Here's what the website administration panel in WordPress looks like:

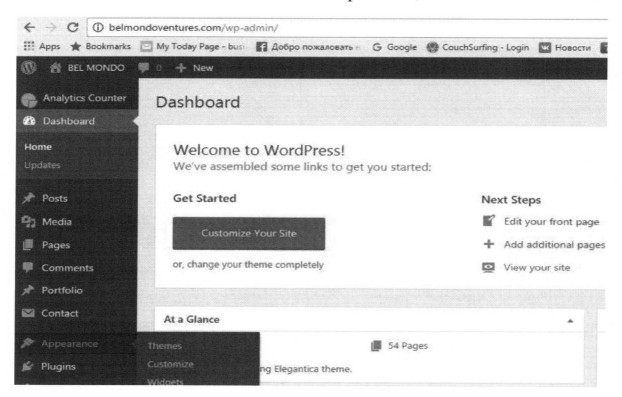

If you cannot cope with this, find an IT volunteer in your city who can help you with the basic setup of the site. Also, I recommend you use the ready-made templates library at themesforest.net. If you are new to designing websites, pay attention that the template comes with detailed installation instructions. You can also order a cheap website from freelancers, for example, at fiverr.com.

It is useful to create the following pages on your web site: About Us, How It Works, Services / Products, and Contact Us. For the content of the site, use the material you created for the commercial offer developed in the last chapter.

There should not be any single mistake on your website! Everything has to be right and tight. Any error immediately reduces the impression of your professionalism to zero. Better to keep it simpler but high quality!

Your contacts, or the "Contact Us" page should be visible at a glance on the site because, in the end, you just want to use the site to ensure customers and partners have found you and can reach out to you easily.

Also, it is useful to create a "Blog" section, where you can publish weekly news or your reflections. A blog is a good tool for promotion, because it has original content that allows you to engage your audience with the right keywords. Moreover, people like to read the personal stories of others, so do not be shy when writing about your progress and sharing it in social networks.

It is also useful to create a page on the most popular social networks - Facebook, Instagram, YouTube, and others.

It attracts more attention if you have a short video of 1-2 minutes. This can be a general video about your company, product promo, or video reviews. If you cannot order a professional video, then at least try to make a video with a beautiful background.

6. Colour Palette

The colour palette requires you have a set of primary colours which will be used in all your marketing materials: on the web site, in the pitch, in a logo, headers, office decor elements, business cards, and other documents. Having an agreed upon colour palette allows you to create a professional image of your company for free.

7. Business Card

A business card is also very easy to create with the help of canva.com tools. Define which styles of business cards you like the most and recreate something similar. Business cards will be useful for you in all meetings related to your business. Treat them with care.

☐ I have successfully developed the brand of my business and created a web site!

Chapter 8
ON PARTNERS

If you want to build a system - use the right bricks

If you were not a lazybones in performing the previous tasks of this book, then you already have a trump card - the list of companies interested in your product or service. Now we can go ahead with building partnerships, and you will have something to offer.

A partnership is a way to start a business without any costs at all, and it is the best way to start any new venture. A partnership is like a Lego on which you can lay down your business. By creating such a system and closing a couple of deals, you will better understand the directions in which to develop your business!

The essence of a partnership is to analyse what resources you lack to conduct your business and then offer a mutually beneficial exchange to those who have them. This way you can bring together all the resources.

Here are the most common types of partnerships:

Marketing: This is when you have a product or service, and your potential partner has an audience to whom you want to offer your product or service. For example, your partner is a renowned recruitment agency, and you wish to offer the services of employment of people with disabilities. In this case, you can offer to the partner to expand its customer base in exchange for using its advertising image, brand, and marketing processes.

Production: This is when you have created your clientele, and your partner has a material resource (machines, equipment, materials, software, or any solution) for the production of products and services. For example, if you want to sew blankets for hospitals, then turn to someone who already sews bedding and has special machinery, skilled employees, and established channels of materials to purchase for this purpose. Perhaps they haven't produce the blankets before, but this will be your offer as a partner - to start the production of new products based on the demand of your clientele. Also, if you need any tools or machinery, even computers to run your business - you can ask if the partner is willing to offer them to you for free upon his own process of equipment modernization. Mind that if you are a small entrepreneur with limited resources - you better pitch for partnership with the same small scale of entrepreneurs. If you want to pitch to bigger scale partners you better come up with a classical proposal, service offering.

Finance: This option is good when you can prove you are able to independently produce and sell your service based on the evidence of your resources or similar experience, but you just do not have enough capital to organize this thing. In this case, you should involve a financial partner / investor. Financial partners for your social venture could be of the following types:

a) A classical investor - a person or organization whose main goal is to make profit. For our business, where profits are reinvested in the creation of a charitable effect, this category of financial partner is not optimal. Be cautious when making a deal with a partner because the investor can control how you are running your business and negate your noble motives, creating a mechanism to obtain the maximum profit instead. For example, you decide to create a portal where you list the most environmentally sustainable companies in your country. The investor may require that the first line of sustainable companies to display are those who gave you the most money in advertising to support your initiative, for example, the oil company that financed your bicycle project. The conclusion is that you need to make sure the mission and objectives of you and your investor are alike. The main financial tool that is used in this category of financial partners is equity/shares in your company.

b) Corporate Partner implementing CSR (Corporate Social Responsibility) program - a company that operates in the same niche as your project and is ready to help you financially, provided that you demonstrate the maximum social and environmental impact on the investment and the maximum outreach of your media campaigns. In essence, the company/corporation contracts you to perform your social initiative and in this way it "outsources" you its CSR. To give you an example, a company is engaged in the manufacturing of electronics, and your project is about recycling electrical appliances and batteries. If the company will take you under its wing by financing you, then it will increase their environmental sustainability by creating a full (closed) cycle of manufacturing. Thereby, the company will increase its investment attractiveness, create a better image, and earn respect of shareholders. Thus, the support of your project will be a profitable investment. To close this deal, you will have to provide a plan and targets for your initiative, and then every month you need to give a report on your progress: on the number of collected batteries, installed bins, people involved, the media coverage, and the costs incurred. Also, you need to place the logo of your partner in all your publications. Bringing in a company as a financial partner is a perfect example of symbiosis, allowing you to fully engage in the implementation of the project, which makes the world a better place, while enjoying the benefits of cooperation with a large company. The main financial tool used in this category of financial partners is a service contract.

c) Patron / Philanthropist / Private Fund / Family Office - these are financial partners whose primary purpose is to maximize the charitable effect of their investment, so you are on the same page with them. These individuals and organizations will most likely agree with you on the mission. However, there are some nuances when working with them:

- many of them have a legal limitation - they can only help non-profit organizations (NGOs). This situation arises due to the fact that in some countries, investment in NGOs reduces their tax burden. If this situation occurs and you do not want to register the NGO - then you should list the existing NGOs working in related fields and partner with them before presenting your project to this type of financial partner.
- these organizations are very conservative and non-public. They aim at preserving their capital and reputation, therefore, finding these organizations and individuals is often difficult, and you need to begin negotiations with a small pilot project proposal.

The main financial tool used by this category of financial partners is a grant, interest-free loan, a contract for services.

d) Institutional Investors - these include the State Agency for Investments, major intergovernmental organizations (UN), and international programs (EU - Horizon2020, EITDigital). Typically, these organizations announce a tender and gather proposals on addressing some challenges (gender equality, promotion of entrepreneurship, green economy projects, etc.). Participants submit their projects in accordance with the prescribed form and terms, and the winners receive support and provide regular reports. The disadvantage of participating in such programs is that they are quite bureaucratic and formalized, i.e., if you have no successful experience of attracting a grant, it is better to not spend too much time doing this and rather cooperate with a partner who has a positive experience. Many of the programs are provided exclusively for NGOs, although with the development of social entrepreneurship, there are more and more programs that support private companies. The main financial tool used by this category of financial partners is a grant, co-investment, or loan.

e) Crowdfunding platforms - while you have several popular platforms in your city or country, foreign platforms include Kickstarter, kiva.org, and many others. The main principle is to attract a little bit of money from a lot of people. This mechanism is most convenient and applicable for the promotion of real products that can be bought as a pre-order. However, it also works well with charitable campaigns. In order to work successfully with crowdfunding, your project should look very beautiful with professional illustrations, and the project description should touch the soul. You will also need to involve the media to speak about and promote your initiative. Crowdfunding can consist of one of two kinds: one type is when you get the money only if the entire amount is collected, and another where you'll get as much money as you gather regardless if the campaign has collected 100% of the intended budget or not.

The main principles of cooperation with partners:

- **Mutually Beneficial.** No matter how wonderful and unique your product or service may seem, you must design a simple, clear-cut proposal with numbers showing how you can bring real, tangible benefits. Tailor the size of your influence to the size of the company you are pitching for.
- **Clear.** You must offer a very clear and transparent plan of action and have the maximum information about how to implement those activities where you are asking for help.
- **Long-term.** Envisage the plan for the development of partnership for at least a year.

To communicate with potential partners, you can use the same database "Potential Partners". For each category, prepare a commercial offer based on the template we have developed.

The lowest efficiency is obtained if you just send out your proposal by email. If you do this, do not expect to an answer. Higher efficiency is to discuss your proposal on the phone. Maximum efficiency is a personal meeting, so do your best to organize it as a personal meeting. You can apply all your creativity and original methods, such as sending a nice letter in the original envelope so it gets delivered straight into the hands of the decision maker, or try to arrange an unexpected meeting outside the office, in a restaurant or at a private event. If this is really important for you, your imagination will give you original ideas of how to make sure you get noticed and appreciated. The main thing is to be yourself, play, have fun, and do not think this is your only chance, but do everything possible to make this chance fruitful.

For the transition of useful legal documents, use a non-disclosure agreement, a letter of intent. This will give your presentation a more professional look. Templates of these agreements can be found on the Internet and you can edit them by yourself for the start.

☐ I made agreements with partners on different aspects of my business! Now I'm sure I have all the resources I need for the successful operation of my business!

Chapter 9
ON THE LEGAL SIDE

Follow the dress code

The legal framework is a set of documents which spell out all the principles of your company's operation and its interaction with partners, customers, and all involved parties. This is your ticket to the world of business, your entrance to the system where you will be able to exchange your goods and services for money.

Here are the main legal issues that an entrepreneur-beginner needs to solve:

1. **Registration of the legal entity;**
2. **Contract with customers;**
3. **Contract with employees;**
4. **Contract with partners.**

Choosing the form of a legal entity

First of all, do not worry about the registration of a legal entity before you are not entirely sure that you have customers, and they expressed a clear intention to work with you. Registering your company can be done within one day in most of the countries, so you can align it with onboarding your first customer.

Step 1: Commercial or non-profit?

There are certain restrictions of activities that can be run by a non-profit company. For example, non-profits in many countries are not allowed to sell any services or produce anything. The legal base in many countries is so that NGOs must exist only at the expense of donations and grants, which are not taxed. If you want to become a social entrepreneur and introduce yourself to real market based economy, then a non-profit company is probably not the best choice for you, unless you already have one. Some entrepreneurs have two companies: an NGO to accept grants donations and a classic company to do production and sales.

Step 2: Sole proprietor or a company?

A sole proprietor is a very good option if you do not plan to hire employees in the near future. Being a sole proprietor (individual entrepreneur) allows you to have a bank account, the ability to enter into contracts, the ability to have a flat tax rate (this depends on a country), and lower running costs. It is not necessary to take office. However, you cannot hire employees. In addition, the status of a sole proprietor suggests that the work will be done by a single professional, i.e. this is definitely the image of a very small business, boutique, or consultancy. Keep that in mind during the negotiations.

If a sole proprietor is not a fit for you, consider other options. The most popular option in most countries will be to register a Limited Liability Company (LLC or Ltd). Generally speaking, limited liability means that when you form a "legal entity" it becomes like a new member of society which responds for its debts only with the capital it has. That means you generally won't be liable for the loss in an amount greater than your share capital, so you won't risk your property in case of debt (unless your property is actually your company's property). Limited liability may also mean that your company is limited to its partners, i.e. outsiders cannot acquire a share of your company.

For start-up companies, it is very convenient to operate under a simplified system of taxation. Most countries have their own offers for start-ups and their guidance on the fastest, cheapest, and most convenient way to get you started. I recommend you consult with your city tax authorities.

Step 3: In order to register a company, you need to prepare a number of documents and submit them to the registering authority. Registering your company normally takes place on the same day your application is submitted.

You would need to choose a legal name for your company. Check beforehand on a special website for your country to see if the chosen name is free. Even if the most best names are already taken, don't worry, because you will not be promoting your company's name, but your brand. You will also need to create a charter for your company. You can search the standard templates or consult an attorney. Also, you might need to get some stamps or signature verification in a specially accredited institution depending on the laws of your country.

Upon the registration, you will receive a special registration number to communicate with the main public services:

- A unique taxpayer identification number - your company's tax identification number;
- Social Security - to deal with salary taxes and pensions;
- Insurance;
- Statistics authorities.

All this really depends on your country or even region or town. Your registering body will consult you on where you need to report and how often.

Step 4: Opening a bank account.

Look for start-up packages with low monthly costs or low costs per single transaction. When choosing a bank, pay attention to customer service packages, how many useful instruments there are, and how many payments, cards, and additional services included.

Nowadays, most banks are equipped with secure and encrypted systems for online or remote transactions without having to visit a bank office. For that, you will be installed or given access to special software and maybe given a special encrypted token.

If you accept payments from individuals, you might need to have special equipment such as registered machines for issuing receipts, or payment terminals. Consult on these topics with your company registering authority and with your bank. If you deal with import/export you must have a foreign currency account, too.

Many countries encourage export and discourage import. That may mean that if you want to buy something from abroad, a special import tax might be added, though this might not be the case for you. And overall, national and local governments execute different programs which provide perks to underprivileged industries, locations, and target groups. For example, there can be tax exemptions if you open a business in a small town with a high rate of unemployment or if you sell on export. Check with your town or country's programs.

Now your company is registered, congratulations!

Contracts with Customers

The legal basis for all your arrangements is the legal framework of your country or of the country whose law you will apply while dealing with your foreign customers. You need to be aware of the legal acts and laws regulating your field of business, so check them out on the internet.

If your clients are individuals, then a contract with them is usually a receipt. Sometimes, in addition to the receipt, you are required to have additional documents, such as terms of service, guarantees, or public offerings. The unspoken rule is that the more expensive the product or service is, the more legal documents are used to cover all possible risks.

No matter what your business is, I recommend you gain the support of corporate customers - legal entities and not just individuals. Cooperation with legal entities normally involves a larger amount of transactions, as well as long-term opportunities. One you sign up, you may provide yourself with a good bulk of orders without having to worry about selling again. This stability is always a good impact on the business because it allows the boss to relax a bit from the constant search for new customers and instead focus on strengthening the product or service. Legal entities are the umbrellas for the whole audience of customers and employees whom you can access through the contract with a company.

The main principle in concluding contracts with customers is to promise less and deliver more. Any promises written in a legal form in your contract are binding, therefore, try to mitigate the amount of liabilities specified in the contract. Try not to constrain yourself with legal promises on timing and volumes, but on your part, do everything possible to please the client. After all, the set of legal documents is just a base that will be used to resolve disputes in court, though of course you should do your best to resolve any issue before court. And the real success of your business is in your devotion to your product quality and the well-being of your clients. Try to find a mutually winning (win-win) option for cooperation as it is the key to long-term relationships.

If you have a single type of customer and one service, the contract will be a standard one for everybody, maybe with only a difference in project plan sections. Look for the contract templates for your activity on the Internet. This will make you aware of the main blocks of issues determined by the contracts in your field of work, and you can edit these templates according to your conditions.

Contracts with Employees

Interaction with employees is governed by the Labour Code of your country. Again, look for typical legal acts and laws on your activity. The contract with your employees is an important link in maintaining the confidentiality of your technology or method. The contract can specify the prohibition for the employee to engage in the same kind of business for several years (non-compete). The agreement also specifies the rate of rewards, positions, and sometimes duties and the corresponding efficiency metrics. As an alternative to working with employees on a standard employment basis, you could also consider working with consultants and freelancers. The difference is that with the consultants you can arrange the payment for the result, i.e. agree on the sum of a payment, which is paid if they achieve their metrics. While with a staff you usually work on the principle of a full day's work, regardless of the results achieved.

Contracts with Partners

In the case where you purchase goods or services, it is important to describe all the minimum requirements for the quantity and quality characteristics of your order. This agreement will be your reason to accept or reject a service or product that you receive.

While working with partners, try to flexibly distribute the financial burden, especially at the start. For example, instead of purchasing a unique software, try to negotiate a contract with payments per session or based on small monthly subscription. Or instead of paying for a full range of marketing services, pay separately for every attracted client or for achieving a specific result expected with the purchase of this service.

With the advancement of IT, there are more and more free or low cost programs aimed at mass usage that you can test first and then move on to a premium plan. Excellent affiliate products that are useful to any small business include software for accounting, software for project management, for task scheduling, quality control, work with objections and questions of customers, software to generate invoices, to create documents, available templates for design and engineering, and more. These programs can significantly automate any business. Contracts with them are a public offer. You can find them in the Google Apps directory or other similar marketplaces.

☐ I turned my venture into a legal entity! I registered my company, concluded a contract with the bank, became listed in the state bodies, and developed contract templates for customers, employees, and partners.

Chapter 10
ON ACCOUNTING AND OFFICE

Down to earth topics keep us grounded

The main task of accountants in our times is to make sure all the regulatory authorities (tax agency, social security, insurance) are satisfied and have no complaints. In some countries, there is an opportunity to conduct business either in a simplified form or full-fledged accounting.

Reports to the regulatory authorities can be on a monthly, quarterly, or annual basis. Research which authorities you must report to with your type of business and what specific forms should be completed for the reports. Nowadays most reports can be generated and transmitted remotely using the appropriate software. Spend some time and learn how to do it yourself, or ask a freelance accountant or specialized accounting company to do it for you either on a one-time basis or by signing an incurring contract. A prerequisite of hiring an accountant or a commercial consultant may exist in your country for your type of activities, check if this applies to you.

Having a good idea of your accounts is also useful for your financial planning. To do this, open your banking software and list all the incoming revenues for the period. Create a pie chart and insert the data of your revenues from different sources or different categories of clients. Then do a similar exercise with the costs. Just look at whom you paid the most to in the selected period and analyse the optimality of these payments. Write down your conclusions on where you see potential for growth in your revenues: should it come from your efforts of bringing in new clients or from the efforts of increasing the average paycheck of existing clients by providing them with better and extra service? Do the same for your costs: would you rather cut some costs or increase some of them because they will provide a really good, vivid return?

Rent

Having an office is a prerequisite for certain types of companies in certain counties. All companies are supposed to have a legal address, that is, the address where official correspondence from the public authorities comes. However, the company may actually be located at a different address. For example, a company can be registered in a small town somewhere in the region, and pay taxes there, but conduct its business in a bigger town.

When you rent an office, make sure there is a legal address available for your use. Not all the offices or spaces meet the requirements for the placement of legal entities. They might not have a sufficient amount of light or temperature control, they may belong to solely residential use, or have other limitations. In many countries, there is the concept of a "virtual office". A virtual office is a place where you are not actually present, but you this address in your contracts and marketing materials. Renting a "virtual address" in London costs about 40 pounds a year.

Price calculations for renting an office are usually carried out at a rate per square meter/ square foot + utility bills. The rental rate of office space can go up and down, so take these dynamics into account in the contract. Do not conclude a contract for more than a year, if you feel the rate could fall. However, in any case, ask the landlord regarding the plans for your space, and whether he plans any major repairs, demolitions, the sale of the building, or other changes that may affect your lease. Also, see if there is extra room in your building in case your small business expands rapidly and requires additional space. Pay attention to the office infrastructure, and whether it has a telephone and internet line, whether it is conveniently located for the staff to commute to the office, and if there are restaurants or shops nearby.

Repairing the office at the start-up phase is quite a risky initiative because you do not know how things will go, and investments in repairing the office usually provide little benefit for business development and take a lot of your time and focus away.

Do not forget to take into account your costs for the purchase of office furniture, computers, and office equipment.

Chapter 11
ON MARKETING

Time to grow over your boundaries

When you have a clear plan, a legal entity, and interested contacts it is time to sell! The selling process should start before the production process in your business! This allows you to distribute cash flow more intelligently, reduce risk, and increase business efficiency. This means that in the beginning you have to do everything to get the order, and then to complete it, and not vice versa. The following types of payment agreements are the most common:

- **Prepaid** - when you get part of the money for the goods immediately at the conclusion of the contract,
- **Upon sales** - when you hand over the goods to the store, and then you are paid for the actual goods sold,
- **Partially** - when a project is broken into milestones and payment comes for the fulfilment of all the conditions for each part,
- **Subscription** - a fixed payment each month.

The best way to sell is not to sell at all, but to share the joy, love, beauty, and other qualities you defined as a part of yourself in the second chapter and which became the basis for your business.

You should always remind yourself that the person making the purchase does not want your product per se, but the feeling or state of harmony, fullness, wealth, and respect which comes with it. So let your product or service always reveal itself in the fullness of its mission, even in the smallest details!

It is time again to call up those contacts who were already interested in your business. When you work with your database of potential customers, take notes of the most frequent objections, anticipate them before they occur, and try to understand what is behind the objection.

Here are typical cases of objections:

"Thank you, but I am not interested" - this refusal doesn't give you any real understanding of what's wrong. You should ask clarifying questions: Have you used such a service in the past? Is it because of the price? Maybe it is more convenient to discuss our proposal later or, for example, over a cup of coffee?

"Too Expensive" - What are you comparing it with? What is your budget for this kind of service? What is the ideal outcome you would like to get for the money? Let's try to work in a test mode, and you will see the quality and value of our proposal.

"We are already working with another supplier" - Could you tell us more about your experiences? Are you always happy with them? Why did you choose them? What prevents you from testing our proposal for the future, given that we have obvious advantages to offer?

Sales is the foundation of any business and I advise you to study this area more profoundly, regardless of your main role in the company. In particular, learn about dealing with objections.

Be kind, gracious, and thankful for the opportunity to have this discussion. Try to bring extra value into the conversation: consult your customer, give them some tips, or at least share an excited, joyful mood.

If you still do not have enough customers to fulfil your plan, you can extend your influence by using marketing tools.

Here are the basic techniques used to attract customers:

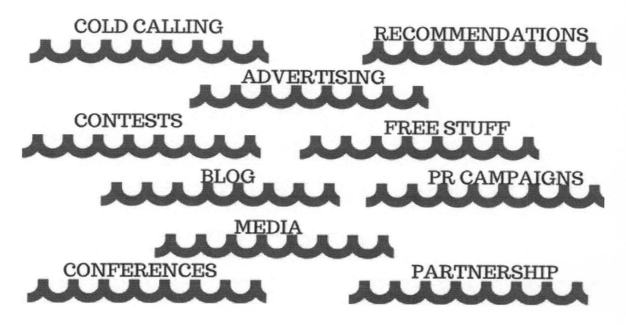

Cold calling is a type of sales technique where you call all the companies in a row from a database of your target customers. Such databases for different types of activities and for different countries are sold on the Internet. The goal of a cold call is to "warm up" a customer's interest so that he becomes open to receive and review a special offer from you by e-mail or even meet in person. In conversations on the phone, try to find out who makes the decisions for your offer in this company and try to communicate with that person directly. However, do not ignore the possibility of communicating with the secretary or an ordinary employee, you can turn them into your allies, explaining how cooperation with you will solve their problems.

References work well after you have delivered the services successfully. Then you may ask them who else might be interested in your offer. Also, you can ask for a direct introduction to a particular person or a company if you know your client has a connection. After providing your service, ask the client to leave feedback about your work and ask whether you can publish it. You can even film a short video reference, which is even more trustworthy! If every customer recommends you to two more contacts, your business will grow exponentially! To achieve this, you must try to maximize the quality of your service so it becomes so demanded and needed you don't need to worry about selling again.

Advertising is the use of a third-party's gathered audience for a particular resource. The audience which you advertise to must exactly match the type of a customer to whom you want to sell. It is better to select a resource with a small audience, but very tailored to the purpose of your business. Also, when dealing with advertising in social networks and Google it is very important to specify the parameters such as audience, age, region, and key interests. Many advertising budgets are wasted simply because they ignoring these simple rules! Any advertising must begin with a test phase to control its efficiency. Promotional text should speak the same language as the customer, have a call to action, and contact information in a visible place. You should not rely too much on advertising, because if customers appears for a short time and then go away the problem is not in sales, but in your business model and your service. It simply does not comply with the wishes and needs of your customer.

Contests are a good way to engage customers in activities and are often carried out on social networks. For the contest, you should already have a subscriber base on your page to ensure the virality thanks to a developed first line (existing subscribers). If you are just beginning, then I suggest you create a contest and publish it in specialized groups on social networks, such as those that only deal with contests. They collect all possible contests and post them on their page. In order to win the prize, players must subscribe to your page, share your page among their friends, and like your post. As a result, you can give the prize to a randomly chosen winner on the basis of the highest number of likes to his post or photo.

Free stuff is a good mechanism to attract attention to your company. There are several particularities to consider. 1) Since you do it for free, do not expect payment. The fact is, there are many veiled free services, for example, when the client is invited to the presentation, where he receives heavy advertisement of products and is provoked into guilt if he doesn't buy. These techniques are not effective as a long-term strategy, because you pay only out of pity, and you certainly will not recommend this to friends. If you do something for free - try to bring in people with a wide range of contacts in your field or bring in bloggers. 2) Make sure that you are able to handle all the "free" customers. Test the percentage of conversion on paid customers on a small sample. Your free bonuses have to bring your business and not put you into debt.

Generally, free stuff works well for information, digital, and marketing industries, where you just make some content available for free and this costs you zero, so customers become familiar with you and subscribe to your paid services.

Blog - This is the section of your web site or a special group in social networks where you write about your business, news, industry trends, promotions, and updates. This original content allows you to appear as a proven expert in your subject and thereby increases your credibility. In addition, blogs with their own unique content occupy the top ranks in the search engines, like Google.

PR campaign - in our case, charitable, social, and environmental effects are the main components of our business. Feel free to widely spread the information about the good deeds you are engaged in, because it helps you and others be inspired and perhaps sometime in the future your readers will also start making the world a better place because they were inspired by you. Believe me, your news is much nicer and more useful than all the garbage information about tragedies, crises, and disasters that our media is stuffed with! Maintain your image with constant news about your progress in achieving social and environmental results. Remember, you are a social entrepreneur - someone very unique, who combines business and charity! The world needs to hear more about you!

Media - Involving the media will allow you to reach to a wider audience. When something important actually happens in your venture - write a press release (special text and images), create a kit, and send it to journalists. Also, if you organize an interesting event - invite journalists to highlight it. Accompany your news with personal, emotional stories, they unite the hearts of people.

Conferences - This is an excellent opportunity to establish direct personal contact with people making decisions. To make use of a conference, you need to be prepared. Rehearse how you will present your business in one sentence. Learn at the website who the delegates are, write down whom you want to meet, establish contact with them in a professional network like LinkedIn, and discuss your intention to communicate in person at the conference. Collect business cards. Send an email to the person you met immediately after the meeting to remind them about yourself and set a good tone. A week after the conference, call all the contacts. Do not skip the informal part of the conferences - the party. Sincere conversations that grow business cooperations often happen there.

Partnership - The best way to sell is to delegate this activity to partners. Find companies with similar services and convince them to make a separate page on their website with a description of the special services provided by you. Also, put forth your best effort to be on the shelves of large retail chains. Having done this once, you will have the foundation of permanent contracts, which is a constant source of revenue. Make it so that your business could be transferred to other locations: prepare the franchise documentation and instructions, and find a partner who wants to deploy your business in a new location. Indicate on your website the phone numbers of your partners in different regions and pay them a commission on sales.

Make the first sales yourself so you know for sure what works in your business, and only then should you delegate this activity to sales managers.

☐ My sales process works accurately, efficiently, precisely, and with the result as I planned. I can see how I will be able to increase my sales when necessary.

Chapter 12
ON TEAM

Love your people the same as you love yourself

Competent relationships with your team are the key to your business success. The role of a good CEO is to steer your ship in the right direction, to embody the vision, analyse the results of the work in all directions, and spot the trends. An authentic entrepreneur first delegates all possible activities to partners, and those that remain within the company he delegates to employees. However, studies show that not every entrepreneur knows how to delegate and spends much of his time on accounting, sales, work with social networks, and other activities rather than on establishing processes. It is because of this fact their business gets stuck. They overload themselves with business instead of separating from it and therefore have no more oxygen for growth. It is very important to delegate; however, you as an entrepreneur must know how to do everything in your business yourself. Only by having a very good understanding on how to handle a specific area of your business can you successfully communicate it to employees, delegating this area and getting the extra value of their deeper expertise on this topic.

Here are the specific steps for team selection:

Step 1: Go back to Chapter 3 where you created the strategy and tactics for your business. Perhaps with your new developments it is time to update it a bit. Take all the stickers with the description of tactical tasks and divide them into small groups according to the number of people you intend to hire - these will be the tasks for the employees. Align these tasks based on their priority. A start-up usually takes one person for each of the key areas. For example, one person will be fully responsible for all the tasks on marketing, the other on the product, and the third on finance and accounting, etc.

Step 2: Write down a job description, requirements for the candidate, and tasks. See if you require practical experience for each particular role or if it is enough for the person to simply desire to learn. Look at which areas you can actively train employees, and where you expect profound knowledge on their side. If you have strong experience in different aspects of your business, you can take people without experience as students, but make sure they are people who are very aligned with your spirit, and teach them everything from scratch. In this way you will have a predictable, result driven team, and low costs by hiring newbies.

Step 3: Make sure you have sufficient financial resources for the maintenance of your team, at least for a few months. If resources are not enough, then your option is to suggest that a suitable employee share the risk with you and become your partner. Remember, you need to invite employees only at the time when there is reasonable assurance that the product and service is selling well. Try to earn a little revenue on your own and spend the money on a specialist who will close the most critical issues at this stage of your business. If you are very constrained financially take employees on a part time basis or just on an assignment for a single task. Perhaps, if your financial needs to start are high enough, you will need to find an investor, sponsor, or an incubator. For information on how to do this, go back to Chapter 8 "Partners". Try to do everything possible to reduce your financial burden, simply give away a part of the processes in your business at the mercy of your partners. Mind your very narrow field from the start. Believe me, it is much more healthy to start small and then expand rather than start with a debt and big ambition in your head. When you stand strong on your feet - then you can grow your business in breadth or in depth if you would like.

Step 4: Publish an ad with your job offer on a specialized web site, and appoint interviews. Keep your clarity in mind about the most important things you are looking for in employees, and what is secondary. This applies to both professional and personal qualities. At the same time, be open to learning something new and unexpected from the candidates, something that will give you a fresh look at your business.

In addition to the evaluation of employees by their primary functional responsibilities, the boss must have a certain disposition to understand the emotional state and aspirations of employees.

For example, if an employee is always very quick in performing his/her tasks and exactly in the manner as you ask, no less, no more - it is the quality of an executive, who himself can manage multiple employees. Such a person does not delve into the essence of the issues and works on the expected result. Such a person can be quite lazy, and at the same time very clever. He will find a way to solve his tasks as quickly as possible or "outsource", delegate, and control. You can gradually raise the bar for such an employee and, accordingly, the bonuses for the result.

If an employee is always very worried about his/her jobs and does everything carefully, is emotionally involved, and takes time studying new information in his/her field - he/she is a performer you can really rely on. Such people are able to build your rear and keep you out of trouble on important things. These people can be entrusted with the job of accounting, law, editing, and quality control. People with this character trait should not be pressured or hurried, because they are not the fastest people by definition, but their strong point is that they are not willing to compromise on quality. Any pressure will just create futile stress for them, these people feel relaxed while working in their rhythm.

If you have a sceptic person on your team this is usually the specialist who has the talent to analyse the situation and suggest the improvement of certain components of your business or overall mastering. Determine with him/her what task he/she intends to solve, give him/her a time, and leave them alone, do not control every step. When the time comes, analyse the results together. However, there are different types of sceptical people. Make sure your employee is an authentic person, and not a manipulator who is trying to sabotage your decisions and take time off from tasks and discourage the team. You do not need people on your team with whom you do not share a common vision. They demoralize the staff. If you have such a case it is better to stop the cooperation with such a person, but understand this situation is your fault and your failure to understand the real needs and talents of a particular person.

If you have an entertaining, merry person on your team direct them to communicate with other people, look for clients, and work in social networks. Also, such an employee will be an excellent psychologist for your office - just ask him/her what the issues and problems of the members of the team are and how he/she would propose to resolve them.

These are just some of the examples. Watch the qualities of your employees as they appear and see in what capacity they can be used at their best. If you can create a harmonious team where everyone is at his place your business will grow easily and quickly. Also, as a leader, always understand that the responsibility is always on you. If something does not work then this is your fault; it means you did not manage to teach properly, select and control properly, or voice your conditions. Maybe you even disregarded the claims of your employees. The boss must always be in balance, this allows you to simply watch over everything that is going on and make decisions aimed at harmonization and growth.

For managing HR, I suggest you use special software for task scheduling on daily or monthly basis (for example, Insightly), for joint work on projects (e.g. Trello), and for writing reports (I use Google Docs).

☐ I created a perfect team. My team is able to resolve all the challenges of our business and loves their work.

Chapter 13
ON FINANCE

Let the blood circulate

This is the most pragmatic chapter in this book. Finances are the blood of the economy. People are willing to give you money for what brings them even greater value. If your work does not create cash flow it likewise does not bring value. You can argue long and hard about people's inability to comprehend your deep nature, about your non-systemic thinking, about the corruption and dishonesty of everyone around you, about karma and the unfairness of life - but this is just a pointless bluff of your ego and an attempt to comfort yourself. The fact remains obvious - you have no money, there is no adequate return for your work. Does this mean that you're not talented? No! Does this mean that the case you chose may not be profitable? Not at all!! Does this mean you are not educated enough and knowledgeable in all the matters of your business? Yes. But at least you are on the right track! It is likely that your chosen path is unbeaten and not easy, but the reward and satisfaction shall be appropriate. Keep your faith. The system is logical and unemotional for all participants. If someone has success in a certain aspect, for example, financial - this means that person has done something very logical for the system to answer, YES! Even the most awkward beginnings for some people lead them to success. It can be the same for you.

Though you will not go far based only on the idea of your excellence, you must be able to use all the tools that play a role in your industry and add quality. Here we are talking about investing. INVESTING is a process of spending your time, money, and labour on something that benefits the business. Note, it benefits not you personally, but your business. Although, if you follow the methodology of this book, it is all about determining the business of your soul, and what is good for your soul will automatically be good for your business. Soon you will see how this works in finance. Now do you understand why we figured out your mission in the second chapter and tried to create such a mechanism where you and your business are one single unit?

If you aim for growth and development you need to invest in assets.

Assets are what directly contribute to the growth of your business performance.

Here is an example of assets and liabilities for the business of an IT studio that develops websites:

Assets	Liabilities
Designing a website; Purchasing website templates for clients; Getting knowledge about advertising for IT; Ads purchase; Running webinars on websites management; Purchase of hosting, etc.	Office with expensive design; Automobile; A trip to a foreign country to relax; Purchase of new dresses;

Now let's look at an example of another business. *Here is an example of the assets and liabilities for a YouTube channel which films trips to exotic countries and donates a part of the profit to supporting local social initiatives.*

Assets	Liabilities
Trip to an exotic country to relax;	Creation of own mini-YouTube

Purchase of new dresses;	platform;
Investing in knowledge about advertising in YouTube;	Creation of own network of advertisers;
Ads purchase;	Office with expensive design;
Creation of own video content;	Automobile;
Study of culture of other countries.	

Conclusions:

Conclusion 1: Something that is equal to death for one business is the ticket to life for another business.

Conclusion 2: When you work on something you do not love, you need to always spend your resources, time, and effort on something you do not love. This creates a logical dissonance. A person tries to pursue his/her business based only on his/her will power. The person tries to dedicate all the effort to business and then somehow restore himself/herself in their free time so he/she can invest again this fresh energy in the business he/she does not love. The person tries hard to find the solution of this situation, for example, by abstracting, by not getting involved too much, by calling it "just work", "everybody works and I do", "only 8 hours and then I am free", by conducting the job mechanically, without involving his/her soul. The diagnosis for these people is a robot, zombie, or a slave. Even a businessman is not far from these categories if he managed to earn a lot, but sacrificed even more. That is a businessman with the illusion of freedom and happiness, who spends a lot of money on entertainment to regain his happiness and joy.

The alternative situation is when you're having fun doing what you love and what is also your business is your asset. For example, you love to travel and you go travelling to Burkina Faso, where you also buy local outfits. This contributes to the success of your business and of you personally, though, for example, if you ask your neighbour Vasya who is a programmer and a geek, this plan would be torture for him. He would rather program for 12 hours a day.

Now it is your turn to define which of your costs are clearly the assets and which are liabilities. Your business is like a child who needs to be fed to grow up. The same is true with respect to assets, you feed your business, so please feed it exclusively with something that contributes to its growth. Let's be honest - it is not necessary to add an expensive office and repair to "assets" unless you have 100 people a day entering your office. Do not try to justify that an expensive new outfit or office will allow you to better tune in, to feel more organized, or get more attention from partners - these are ungrounded and very emotional arguments. And most importantly - it is an investment in you, not in your business. It is your personal problem that you cannot concentrate, not your business's. Our goal for today is not to entertain ourselves, but to develop our business and quickly bring it to the level of stability of financial indicators which will then allow you to pamper yourself. Make it so your "liabilities" column remains empty at the start. Determining your liabilities is very simple - write down what you spend the most money on right now and what the real benefit you get from this investment is. If that is expensive and of little use, then this is a liability of your business. Get rid of it and feel the freedom.

Table "Assets and liabilities of my business". Save this table in your

Finance folder.

Assets	Liabilities

In the top lines of your table, write down the assets that immediately give you a guaranteed cash back, and in the lower lines write down the investments which bring your service or product to a new level.

One of the most reasonable investments is in knowledge. When investing in knowledge, choose a trusted expert, who himself/herself reached the result you want. Now there is a lot of the content available in free access on any topic, so at the start you should invest your time (not money) in self-education. These basic materials allow you to test the most common ideas and techniques that lie on the surface. Implement everything you learn in practice, otherwise it is just wasted time. Only later, with the growth of your own EXPERTISE should you switch to expensive educational materials that can generate an additional return on investment.

Take small steps between investments in the fields of marketing-product-finance-employees. Investing a bit in marketing will bring you two new clients. Invest the revenue from these two clients in the product. Then invest the revenue again in that advertisement that worked and receive five new customers, and so on.

With the proliferation of your cash flow, you can broaden and deepen your investment in your business.

For example, if you want to open a printing shop, there is no need to buy that exclusive printing machine at once. Find the first customer who is willing to pay. Advertise your unique product offer on the Internet, collect the requests and advance payment, and give the order to another company which has that exclusive printing machine. Collect your revenue and invest it once again in attracting customers. When you earn enough to buy the equipment - then buy it. That will be the right time, when you are already an expert in this business and this investment will truly increase your margins with the high probability that you will be able to handle your business while keeping risks under control.

Revenues (permanent and one time) and costs (permanent and one time)

The general formula is that permanent revenues should be as high as possible, while permanent costs should be as low as possible. Therefore you need to do everything so your customer becomes a regular one and your contract becomes long-term. At the same time, you should not bind yourself with fixed costs until there is stability and predictability in your business.

Your base and starting point should be your revenue. In this book, I described how you can start a business without any investment. Your result of completing all the given exercises should be a list of customers who are ready to pay a specific amount for your goods and services. If these clients are not there yet - read through the book again and complete all the exercises. Your revenues must always be at least a little higher than your costs. This is necessary to make ends meet.

So, create a plan of your revenues and costs for the next month and for the coming three months based on your resources and agreements.

Example:

Revenues (+)	Costs (-)
Service for the client A - 500 USD; Service for the client B - 500 USD. Total: 1000 USD.	Salary for the employee to provide the service - 500 USD per month. My personal costs and needs - 200 USD. Service to the boarding house as a charity for free - 0 USD. Purchase of the materials for the service to clients A, B, and the boarding house - 200 USD. Communication with journalists, writing an article about us - 0 USD. Total: 900 USD.
Total: +100 USD.	

In our example, the provision of services to the clients A and B is a one-time service. Therefore, we should try to turn them into permanent customers. For example, think of accompanying services, of teaming up with a partner to provide parallel services for this target audience, developing support, customer service offers, and others. Also, ask for a good review and the recommendation of the client, and do everything to ensure the client is satisfied. A good review will be your asset earned, and it will eventually generate profits and return on investment. Getting a recommendation is a free opportunity to offer your service to a potential client.

With regard to costs, the wage of an employee in the example and your own monthly costs are fixed costs. Carrying out social campaigns and procurement of the material are variable costs that grow in line with the clientele.

How can we optimize fixed costs? As for the employee - you can find someone who is willing to perform the work on a project basis. In this case it is not necessary to keep the person on staff and pay their salary and salary taxes regardless of the amount of work. Typically, a single project work is 10-50%, or sometimes even 100% less expensive than having a person on staff, so when you reach a stable order volume you can hire a specialist, and if he still has a lot of free time - you can delegate the part of the tasks with the closest scope, for example, tasks on the development of your core product. You can also hire someone part-time. It is advisable to discuss your situation directly with the employee and come together to a working model.

With regard to the costs of implementing your social mission and of the achievement of the social effect as it was originally included in the strategy of your company, one of the main objectives is to maximize your social and environmental effect. Social effect also gives a lot of bonuses to the business - it is a source of free advertising by attracting journalists and building loyalty in your employees. However, even in your approach to maximizing social impact it is useful to think in terms of "return on investment", questioning yourself on how you can spend less but maximize the efficiency of the result. For example, you are doing a training. So instead of holding many classes in different locations - you can record videos and agree with the management that they will be viewed together with the children, or you can transfer the training manual with your knowledge to your graduates, ambassadors, or evangelists of your ideas.

As a result of our example, it turns out that we made a profit of 100 USD, and at the same time, a social action was carried out, which in addition to its main social purpose will also increase interest in our business and bring new clients. Thus, the profit can be invested, for example, on automation or writing guidelines on the service so it takes less effort and time in future. Therefore, you should strive to untwist the wheel, where the revenue goes into the costs and allows more revenue to come.

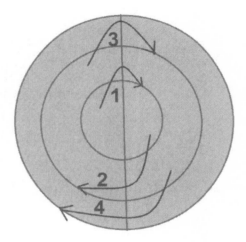

Figure 1: The process of unwinding the cycle "revenues - costs".

Now fill in the table with your plan for the next month. Then, fill in another table designed for the next three months, and hang it in a prominent place. Be realistic and start with the resources and facts that are already established.

Revenues (+)	Costs (-)
Total	

The Cost of Business

If you lack the finances to conduct your business, you need to attract it by demonstrating transparently where the money is buried in your business. Also, it is good to know the value of your business if you want to sell it and move on to something else.

The value of the business is the value of its assets, i.e., the components that are like cows that yield milk without requesting much. In order to present your business to an investor, make sure you have created some of these assets. The more, the better:

Audience/Market - the number of potential customers whom you can sell to. For this asset, you can display the number of subscribers to your web page or your social networks and their involvement; the number of customers whom you called and who gave you a preliminary "yes"; the number of contacts of people who have already bought something similar.

Content - the structured material that can be sold to someone. For example, a large number of photos on certain subjects; a large database of contacts from your niche; a large number of written blog posts, methodologies, and books on the subject; marketing research with detailed answers from your audience and its analysis.

Product or machinery - something tangible that can be profitable. This includes machinery, materials supply, software licenses, cars, computers, instructions, designs, and streamlined production processes.

Finance - liquid/disposable financial resources as well as the financial results and forecast for their growth with the leverage of investment.

Team - a group of people with the necessary knowledge and unique competence that can implement this thing.

Your job as an entrepreneur is to maximize these assets, then you can exchange them for investment.

To sum up, the main task in financial planning is to understand which part of your business has a hole (marketing, product, finance, team, or administration), to find an effective and guaranteed solution while testing the various options, and direct the means to address the issue until the planned result is achieved. Your business must have harmonious financial growth, which means the business has to grow at the pace of your revenue with the margin. Also, the business itself has to grow in a balanced way, which means a little bit of marketing, then a little bit of product. Do not think an investment like getting an MBA is the most profitable investment for the answer to the hard question like "where to find a buyer for the three ecological rooftops that I produce."

Scale up your business based on the growing and multiplication of your assets until a time when you create a mechanism that provides good income for you and at the same time implements your social mission.

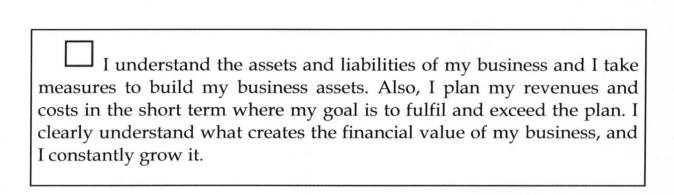 I understand the assets and liabilities of my business and I take measures to build my business assets. Also, I plan my revenues and costs in the short term where my goal is to fulfil and exceed the plan. I clearly understand what creates the financial value of my business, and I constantly grow it.

Chapter 14
ON AUTOMATION

Your baby is already grown up

If you perform all the tasks set out in this book consistently, then you already have a working operating system of your business: sales are happening, the product or service is produced, finance circulates and increases, and the team is working cohesively. You as a leader observe this whole factory. It is important to maintain this detachment of a strategist and just watch the spinning flywheels of the process you started.

The process of launching your business venture is very emotional and labour intensive, but when the signs of stability are present, do not intervene in your established process, trying to do everything on your own and from scratch. Your goal is to develop a working model by building partnerships, delegating tasks, and selecting effective tools.

Review your venture again and direct your energy to its weak points.

As your business grows, you should observe that your revenue and, correspondingly, your profit grows and that your personal time is released. Define for yourself the desired result for your income and for your free time. For example, in my case, I was comfortable with the system when I worked for two weeks per month and had two weeks of traveling. In some of my travels, I combined leisure and business by scheduling meetings with potential buyers in new countries. My goal has never been to expand the business and hire a lot of people, on the contrary, I liked to have as little risk as possible and limited responsibility, and worked on maximizing my profit per hour of involvement.

Look back at the fourth chapter of this book and see if your plan has been executed, both in terms of profitability and social and environmental effects.

Now it's time to once again review your strategy and tactics, erase what does not work and create a detailed description of what does work. This means we need to create a methodology for the deployment of your business in new communities.

Create and fill in the following table, here is an example:

Field	Instrument	How it works
Marketing	Calling the companies from the database	Buy the database of the target industry, Make 20 calls per day, send out a pitch. Just sending out a pitch without a preliminary call doesn't create any conversion.
	Monthly newsletter for regular customers providing special prices.	Brings on average 5 new leads in a day of the newsletter.
	Ads at a specialized platform xyz.com	Brings on average 10 leads per month.
Product	...	...
	..	..
Finance	...	...
	...	..

Fill in the table accordingly, writing down the best practices of your venture and save this table in your "Administration" folder. In the column

"Fields", use some fundamental parts of your business.

It will be useful to create detailed instructions for each area of your operation. Such a formalization and instructions will be the part of your assets, because they can enable any entrepreneur to repeat your success. In addition, it will make your business non-dependent on specific employees or vendors, but dependent on the specific knowledge, tools, and processes you document.

By creating such a model, we are in fact automating the entire process of creating your business. It turns out we are creating a social franchise. Of course, not all mechanisms are universally applicable everywhere, because your business exists within a particular cultural, economic, and other systems. However, many of the principles will work the same way.

Our task today is to find partners and entrepreneurs in other countries who want to repeat your success under your brand or under their own.

My company BEL MONDO Ventures helps goodmakers such as you to prepare franchise documentation of their social start-up and find partners abroad. This service is free and only requires your time. In addition, we create a social incubator for young entrepreneurs, selecting the projects with the highest social and environmental effects and providing them with all the necessary information and resources. The projects will be implemented in Eastern Europe, in Belarus. This location will greatly reduce the costs of the most risky initial phase of business start. The projects that reach success will be introduced in other countries. We are looking for sponsors for the creation of the incubator. The entry investment starts at $1000 and up. So, if you want to try yourself as an investor, and not just a simple investors, but impact investor – you are welcome to co-create with us!

I wish you that as a result of this chapter you will pack your project in a pretty box with a red ribbon. This will be a gift which you will use every day in your business and that can also be useful to others.

No matter if your business is already smooth or still very challenging, the path you are walking is the best out of all options. You are on a quest of building a life where every moment is devoted to your favourite occupation, where working is fun, it fills you with energy, well-being, and pleasant wishes from people whom you help! When you build the system, it is really up to you in what area of your business you want to be active: maybe you delight in making your product with your own hands; maybe you desire to travel and see the world; maybe you enjoy counselling the people in need of your help, maybe you wish to focus on creating comfort in your home, or devote time to sports... I congratulate you with the status of being the creator of your life!

☐ I created and automated the business I love. It makes the

world a better place and it can work even without my involvement. My venture can be implemented in other regions and countries.

I am the creator of my life and always do what I choose and enjoy.

Chapter 15
WE ARE ONE

Just do your best and Thank You

If you dream and act in the direction of doing things you love and help others, I am sure you are a wise and strong person who understands much about life. If you are doing the things you love, you are a successful person. You are successful because you enjoy your activities, and this fills other people with energy and love, and what else in life can be more important and more interesting? If you have not reached the results you dreamed of for your business it just means you have shortcomings in some aspects to work with, maybe in marketing, maybe in finance or team management, maybe with the vision of your product and services, or in the ability to concentrate on your business and work systematically. However, all these limitations can be worked out by obtaining additional knowledge and training. The main thing is that you are on the right track!

Even alone by yourself you can do a lot of good for yourself and for others. But let's talk about us, goodmakers, as a community of people with common interests and objectives to improve the world around us. Wouldn't it be nice if everyone loved their work? In my opinion, this would immediately solve all the problems in the world, and the world would be beautiful. Believe me, it is the desire of everyone to be happy, to be valued at his/her true potential, and be useful to others. Some people are only in the beginning of the way. They are like hedgehogs in the fog, but they do feel that they need something to strive for, though they are not sure how to do it, and whether it is necessary at all...

As experienced goodmakers, let's help these people. Let's support them morally, removing the load of fears off their shoulders and building confidence that they are doing something very interesting and meaningful. Let us share our knowledge with them, something that we believe ourselves that works. It is better not to waste time. Join with them to discuss their plans of turning their ideas to life. Let's help them with resources and contacts. I am sure we will be rewarded nicely. We will have no need to build a high fence, defending ourselves from our neighbours, because they will also be the creators of their little paradise. We will not have to spend much effort on helping people who experience suffering because we can show by example how to suffer less. We will not have to deal with people who are constantly trying to prove their worth because their importance will be obvious by default, manifesting in their love and their joy.

Let's you and I agree that when we reach realization in our business, we help **two** people to also realize their intention. And if everyone does the same, it will create a huge wave of multiplying and an exponential effect! Once upon a time there lived a wise man who provided great service to the king. The king in return wished to generously thank the sage and asked him what he wanted. The sage asked for only **one grain of wheat** to be placed in a cell of a chessboard, and asked to give him two times more grain for each subsequent cell. "That's all?" the king asked perplexedly and fulfilled the desire of the wise man. Here is 1 grain, 2, 4, 8, 16, 32, 64, 128, 256, ... When the cells reached 32, the count of grains was already measured in a ten-digit number and that was only half the board. The number of grains in the 64th cell reached 9223372036854775808, and the total amount of grains of all cells - 18446744073709551615. Such an amount of grain was not even at the disposal of the king! Fortunately, there are only about 7 billion people in the world, and if the spark of our love, respect, and support affects only two people and continues spreading further, than a joyous outcome is inevitable!

☐ I intend to be a social entrepreneur, to solve burdening social and environmental problems, and to provide a good living for myself and my family.

☐ I'm ready to listen to the views of all the people and organizations who want to help me in the development of my business.

☐ When I achieve success, I intend to pass on my knowledge, skills, and resources to two more people who want to become social entrepreneurs. I will do everything possible so that they also become successful and pass on their knowledge to others.

About the Author

Elena Lori (Kozlovskaya) was born and raised in the city of Minsk, Belarus. Her family created the conditions for her intellectual development and motivation to succeed. As a teenager, at 16 years old, Elena entered the business world selling cosmetics. After that, she tried herself in other industries, dealt with construction materials, marketing services, organized a dance school, delivery service, instant tanning, computer repair, engaged in the preparation of business plans, and the sales of IT services. However, this activity did not bring her any success. In 2012, Elena founded her own IT company, which allowed her to travel while pitching the services of her company in different countries and exploring the world. In this way Elena visited more than 60 countries. However, at the time when things seemed to be going smoothly, Elena realized it was still not enough and not even close to her real potential. Her soul looked for more answers. This call made her think more profoundly about the meaning of life and the search of the way. The state of bliss, eureka, and nirvana came on suddenly and confirmed the simple truth about the beauty of every single moment, self-love, and respect to all people. It brought a deep state of calmness along with the joy and perceptiveness of life. Elena's dream is very simple and childlike - she wants all people to be happy, healthy, and prosperous. With this intention, she founded the company BEL MONDO Ventures with the aim of uniting and helping people who are also willing to make the world more beautiful.

Elena is a CEFE certified coach on entrepreneurship. She attended a variety of courses on social entrepreneurship and sustainable development in Belarus and Europe. Elena graduated from high school with honours and has a degree in International Economic Relations from the Belarusian State Economic University.

"If you need an additional consultation or coaching to get you unstuck with any of the topics described - contact me at elena@belmondoventures.com.

Best of luck with your venture and in your life in general. Thank you for making our world more beautiful!" - Elena (the Author)

Made in the USA
San Bernardino, CA
21 December 2018